Uniquely
Montana

Mary Boone

Heinemann Library
Chicago, Illinois

© 2004 Heinemann Library
a division of Reed Elsevier Inc.
Chicago, Illinois

Customer Service   888-454-2279

Visit our website at www.heinemannlibrary.com

Designed by Heinemann Library
Printed in China by WKT Company Limited.

08 07 06 05 04
10 9 8 7 6 5 4 3 2 1

**Library of Congress
Cataloging-in-Publication Data**

Boone, Mary, 1963–
Uniquely Montana / Mary Boone.
    v. cm.—(Heinemann state studies)
Includes bibliographical references and index.
Contents: Uniquely Montana—Climate and
weather—Famous firsts—State symbols—History &
people—Big sky country—State government—
Culture—Food—Folklore and legends—Sports—
Business and products—Attractions and landmarks.
ISBN 1-4034-4648-2 (lib. bdg.)—ISBN 1-4034-
4717-9 (pbk.)
1. Montana—Juvenile literature. [I. Montana]
I. Title. II. Series.

F731.3.866 2004
978.6'01—dc22

2003025476

Cover Pictures

Top (left to right) Montana state flag,
grizzley bear, Custer National Battlefield,
portrait of Chief Joseph **Main** Glacier
National Park

Acknowledgments

Development and photo research by
BOOK BUILDERS LLC

The author and publishers are grateful to the
following for permission to reproduce copyright
material:

Cover photographs by (top, L-R): Todd
Gipstein/Corbis, Robert Holmes/Corbis, Robin
Prange/Corbis, Bettmann/Corbis, Phil
Scheermeister/Corbis

Title page (L-R): Courtesy of University of Montana,
Courtesy of U.S. Geological Survey, Popperfoto/
Alamy; p. 5 Joe Sohm/Alamy Images; p. 6 Courtesy
of U.S. Geological Survey; p. 7 Phil Scheermeister/
Corbis; pp. 8, 14 Courtesy of Alan Applebury;
p. 10 Sinclair Stammers/Photo Researchers; p. 11T
Carol Dixon/Alamy Images; p. 11B Courtesy of
Nation Master; p. 12 Todd Gipstein/Corbis; p. 13
Courtesy of Net State; p; 15T Martin Bache/Alamy
Images; p. 15B Peter Llewellyn/Alamy Images;
p. 16T Robert Holmes/Corbis; p. 16B Doug Wilson/
Alamy Images; p. 17T Steve Brusatte/University of
Chicago; pp. 17B, 26, 31, 34, 41, 44T Courtesy of
Travel Montana; pp. 18, 23T, 23B, 24 Popper-
foto/Alamy Images; pp. 19, 25 Wayne Mumford;
p. 20 Culver Pictures; p. 21 Robin Prange/Corbis;
p. 22 Bettmann/Corbis; p. 28 Walter Bibikow/
Alamy Images; p.33 Courtesy of Montana Muffins;
p. 35 Russ Widstrand/Alamy Images; p. 36
R. Capozzelli/Heinemann Library; p 37 Courtesy of
University of Montana; p. 38 Courtesy of Montana
State University; pp. 39, 43 Third Eye Images/
Alamy Images; p. 40T, 40B Laurence B. Aiuppy/
Stock Connection Inc./Alamy Images.

Special thanks to David A. Walter of the Montana
Historical Society for his expert comments in the
preparation of this book.

Every effort has been made to contact copyright
holders of any material reproduced in this book.
Any omissions will be rectified in subsequent
printings if notice is given to the publisher.

Some words are shown in bold, **like this.**
You can find out what they mean by looking
in the glossary.

Contents

Uniquely Montana

Unique means uncommon. It is a label reserved for people, places, and things with unusual or distinct characteristics. Montana's combined history, climate, geography, and wildlife make it unique. It was the first state in the country to elect a female senator and it is the only state that has rivers that drain into the Gulf of Mexico, Hudson Bay, and the Pacific Ocean.

NAMED FOR MOUNTAINS

When Montana was still a **territory,** governor J.M. Ashley chose the name "Montana." The word comes from the Spanish word *montana* and the Latin word *montanus,* both meaning mountainous. Montana has many mountains. More than half the state is more than 5,000 feet above sea level.

MAJOR CITIES

About 905,000 people live in Montana. Only six states, Delaware, South Dakota, North Dakota, Alaska, Vermont, and Wyoming, have smaller populations. Montana's population density is 6.2 people per square mile. Compare that to Illinois, where the population density is 223 people per square mile.

Helena is both the capital of Montana and the **county seat** of Lewis and Clark County. Located in west central Montana in the foothills of the Rockies, Helena has a population of 25,780. It is a charming **Victorian** city filled with historic homes and locally owned retail shops. Helena's downtown pedestrian walking mall is a popular park-like shopping area featuring historic sites and a va-

riety of shops, coffeehouses, and restaurants. The city's community spirit is seen at its many street festivals, fairs, rodeos, concerts, and plays, such as the annual Last Chance Stampede & Fair.

Missoula is located in western Montana, 45 miles from the Idaho border. It is called the "Garden City" because its winters are milder than those in the rest of the state. The city inspired the novel and movie *A River Runs Through It.* Missoula's artistic, historic, and cultural communities combine to create a unique urban personality. Missoula is home to hundreds of artists, artisans, poets, writers, and actors. The Missoula Art Museum offers twelve to sixteen exhibitions annually in three galleries. The Historical Museum at Fort Missoula has more than 17,000 objects in its collection. A Carousel for Missoula is the first hand-carved carousel built in the United States in the past 60 years. It is located in Caras Park, a downtown gathering place popular for year-round events on the banks of the Clark Fork River. Recently, Missoula was named the best U.S. city for summer climate by CustomWeather.com and one of the nation's five best outdoor towns by *Outdoor Explorer* magazine

Great Falls is located on rich farm land between the Rocky Mountains to the west and Little Belt Mountains to the east.

Great Falls has a population of 56,690 and is located along the Missouri River in central Montana. The river is one of the country's most important waterways. It supplies the Mississippi River with more than half its water. The Missouri River provides Great Falls with its name. As the Missouri cuts through the city it drops more than 500 feet in a series of rapids and five waterfalls, creating the Great Falls of the Missouri.

Montana's Geography and Climate

Montana is located in northwestern United States and is the fourth largest state in the country. It has an area of 146,316 square miles, making it larger than New York, Mississippi, Pennsylvania, and Connecticut combined. Montana is bordered by four states: Idaho, Wyoming, North Dakota, and South Dakota; and two Canadian provinces: Alberta, and Saskatchewan.

THE LAND

Montana has two main geographic areas, the Great Plains and the Rocky Mountain Region. The eastern two-thirds

The Triple Divide

Montana is known as a **headwaters** state because much of the water that flows to the rest of the nation comes from its mountains. Three of North America's largest rivers, the Columbia, Missouri, and Mississippi rivers, begin on Triple Divide Peak in Glacier National Park. They flow in three different directions, ending at the Pacific and Atlantic oceans, and at Hudson Bay.

Montana's mountains vary in size depending upon their age and how they were formed. A mountain's elevation and soil will influence the types of plants that can grow there.

of the state is plains country, level lands, often covered with **prairie.** The center of the state is flatter than the mountainous western third.

Montana is home to more than 50 mountain ranges, most of them in the western one-third of the state. The Rocky Mountains are the largest.

Valleys run through Montana's hills and mountains. A valley is a depression in the earth's surface, often formed by water or ice erosion. Valleys in southwest Montana are 30 to 40 miles wide. Valleys in the north are narrower, often just one to five miles wide.

The highest point in Montana is Granite Peak at 12,799 feet. This mountain is located in central Montana, 45 miles southwest of Columbus. The lowest point in the state is located along the Kootenai River in northwest Montana. There, the elevation is only 1,800 feet above sea level.

Montana's Climate

The western and eastern sections of Montana have different climates because of the mountains that divide the two regions. Normally, weather flows from west to east. When jet streams carry clouds into western Montana, the rain-burdened clouds are too heavy to climb over the mountains, and dump their load in the form of rain and snow. The dry, light clouds can easily climb the mountains now. However, when they get to the plains on the east side, they are almost empty, so they drop little rain.

Eastern Montana's climate is classified as Continental. This means there are large differences between summer and winter temperatures. The eastern plains of Montana often have summer temperatures of 100°F or hotter, and it rarely rains. Winter temperatures can drop as low as –30 to –50°F.

The western mountain slopes enjoy a north pacific coast climate. Western Montana winters are mild (15°F is the average low in January) and summers are usually pleasant (75 to 80°F in July and August). The coldest temperature ever recorded in the United States outside Alaska was –70°F. It was recorded at Rogers Pass, Montana, about 40 miles northwest of Helena, on January 20, 1954.

In nearly all parts of the state almost half of the yearly precipitation falls during three months: May, June, and July.

Average Annual Precipitation
Montana

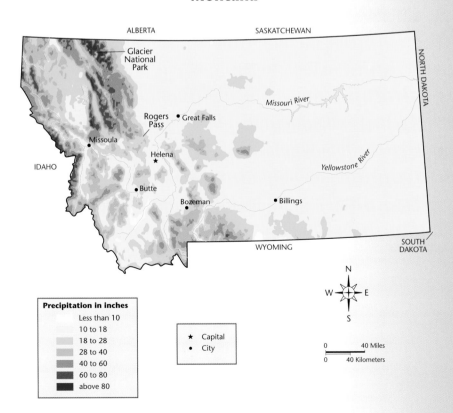

Famous Firsts

More gem **sapphires** are found in Montana than in any other state. In fact, the Gem Mountain sapphire deposit near Philipsburg is one of the largest sapphire deposits in the world. The mountain has produced more than 180 million carats of sapphires since the 1890s.

The first fossil nest of baby dinosaurs and dinosaur eggs found in the world was discovered in 1978 by geologists Marion Brandvold and Jack Horner, at Egg Mountain, near Choteau. As many as 30 million fossils from about 10,000 animals, mostly duck-billed dinosaurs, fill an area more than a mile long and a quarter mile wide. Egg Mountain is located about 100 miles north of Helena.

Flathead Lake in northwest Montana is the largest freshwater lake west of the Mississippi River. It contains 191.5 square miles of water and has 187.6 miles of shoreline. Flathead Lake was carved by glaciers that moved through the area 12,000 years ago. The lake is 28 miles long and spans 16 miles at its widest point.

Yellowstone National Park is the first and oldest national park in the world. It was established on March 1, 1872, by an act of Congress. About 2.8 million people a year explore as many as 10,000 hot springs and **geysers**—more than anywhere else on the earth. The park covers more

Egg Mountain is the world's largest dinosaur graveyard. Scientists believe the dinosaurs buried here were killed when a volcano erupted.

In 1872 President Ulysses S. Grant signed a law declaring that Yellowstone would forever be "dedicated and set apart as a public park for the benefit and enjoyment of the people."

than 2.2 million acres in Montana, Wyoming, and Idaho.

Montana has the largest grizzly bear population in the lower 48 states with between 600 and 800 bears. Grizzlies are protected as a **threatened species** under the Endangered Species Act.

The National Bison Range near Moiese was established in 1908 at the request of President Theodore Roosevelt. It was one of the first wildlife refuges in the nation. The 18,500-acre range is fenced and is home to 350 to 450 bison.

Montana is home to 108 mammal species, more than any other state. Among the state's most well-known mammals are the grizzly bear, moose, wolf, fox, and elk.

The first successful vaccine for whooping cough was developed in 1939 by Dr. Grace Eldering of Meyers. Whooping cough is an infection that causes a bad cough.

Montana's Jeannette Rankin was the first woman to serve in the House of Representatives. She was elected in 1916, at a time when women in most states could not even vote. While in office, she was the only member of Congress to vote against U.S. entry into **World War I** (1914–1918) and **World War II** (1939–1945).

In 1985 a statue of Jeannette Rankin was placed in the U.S. Capitol. Jeannette Rankin was born in Missoula on June 11, 1880. She died in 1973.

Montana's State Symbols

MONTANA STATE FLAG

Montana's state flag is based on a banner Colonel Harry C. Kessler had designed in 1898 for the First Montana Infantry. It was used as an unofficial state flag until its official adoption in 1905. The state name was added in 1981 to make it easier to identify the flag. In 1985 the flag was updated with a new style of lettering.

Montana's first flag is now part of the Montana Historical Society collection.

MONTANA STATE SEAL

Montana's territorial seal was designed by a legislative committee in 1865. Committee members wanted the seal to include the most important symbols of Montana's economy: a plow, shovel, pick, mountains, the sun, the Great Falls of the Missouri River, trees, buffalo, and other wild animals. In 1876, the seal was changed slightly. The buffalo was removed and clouds were added. More changes came in 1887, when the clouds were removed,

A sun setting over snowy mountains, waterfalls, the Missouri River, and trees represents the state's natural beauty. A pick and shovel are symbols of Montana's mining history. A plow stands for its farming history.

• •

trees sprouted where buffalo once roamed, and the sun had shifted position, setting in the west instead of rising in the east. When Montana became a state in 1889, officials continued to use the territorial seal. In 1893, the legislature replaced the word "Territory" with "State" and increased the size slightly.

STATE MOTTO: *ORO Y PLATA*

Oro y Plata is Montana's state motto. The motto "Gold and Silver" originally was suggested because of the area's rich mineral resources. Judge Francis M. Thompson headed up the Montana Territory legislative committee in charge of developing a state motto. He and his committee members thought the saying would sound better in Spanish. Unfortunately, no one on his committee spoke Spanish very well and the group's suggestion to the legislature was "Oro el Plata." Soon a correction was made and the motto became "Oro y Plata."

STATE NICKNAME: BIG SKY COUNTRY

Montana's nickname, Big Sky Country, was first used in 1962. It refers to the way in which the sky often seems to overwhelm Montana's landscape. The name comes from University of Montana graduate Alfred Bertram Guthrie Jr.'s book, *Big Sky*. Montana also has been called the Treasure State, the Bonanza State, Land of Shining Mountains, and the Mountain State.

STATE SONG: "MONTANA"

Montana adopted its official state song, "Montana," in 1935. It was written by Charles C. Cohan and Joseph E. Howard. Cohan, city editor of the Butte newspaper, met

"Montana"

MontanaTell me of that Treasure
   State
Story always new,
Tell of its beauties grand
And its hearts so true.
Mountains of sunset fire
The land I love the best
Let me grasp the hand of one
From out the golden West
Refrain:
Montana, Montana, Glory of the
   West
Of all the states from coast to coast,

You're easily the best
Montana, Montana, Where skies are
   always blue
Montana, Montana I love you.
Each country has its flow'r;
Each one plays a part,
Each bloom brings a longing hope
To some lonely heart.
Bitterroot to me is dear
Growing in my land
Sing then that glorious air
The one I understand.
Repeat Refrain

Howard, a composer, at a gathering in Butte. The two went off to the host's music room and 30 minutes later came back with the basic melody and lyrics of a song. Governor Edwin L. Norris heard the song two nights later and immediately declared "Montana" the official state song. Montana is one of the few states to have a state song and a state ballad. A ballad is different from most songs because it tells a story. The state ballad, "Montana Melody," was adopted in 1983.

STATE FLOWER: BITTERROOT

Bitterroot became Montana's state flower in 1895, but it was important to the state

Bitterroot was rarely eaten raw because of its bitter taste. Early settlers and Native Americans most often boiled the plant's roots and mixed them with meat or berries.

long before that. Bitterroot was treasured as a food by Native Americans and early pioneers. Bitterroot blooms from May to July and grows one-half to two inches tall. The plant likes dry places and is perennial, which means the flower grows back every year.

STATE TREE: PONDEROSA PINE

The ponderosa pine, known as the King of the Forests, became Montana's state tree in 1949. Ponderosa pines can grow 200 feet tall and are found primarily in western Montana.

Early settlers used ponderosa pine to construct buildings. Many timber companies now cut down the trees and turn them into products ranging from lumber to toothpicks.

STATE BIRD: WESTERN MEADOWLARK

Montana adopted its state bird, the western meadowlark, in 1931. The western meadowlark has a broad black "V" on its yellow breast. The bird's back is a mix of brown and black feathers that blend well with its environment. Western meadowlarks defend their territory by singing while perched on tall weeds, posts, or trees. The bird is found throughout Montana. It is popular because of its cheerful song, a loud, clear, warbling whistle.

The western meadowlark's flight is unusual. It alternates rapid wing beats with gliding.

Adult grizzlies weigh as much as 1,500 pounds and can stand up to 9 feet tall. Only Alaska has more grizzly bears than Montana.

STATE ANIMAL: GRIZZLY BEAR

In 1983, the grizzly bear was named Montana's official state animal. More than 55,000 students from 425 Montana elementary schools took part in the selection process. They chose 74 different animals native to Montana, made posters, designed bumper stickers, and held elections. When students finally voted, the grizzly bear received twice as many votes as the elk.

STATE FISH: CUTTHROAT TROUT

Governor Thomas Judge signed a law that made the cutthroat trout Montana's official state fish in 1977. There are many kinds of trout, but the cutthroat trout was chosen because it is a native fish that is in trouble. Some environmental groups have asked to list them as a **threatened species** under the Endangered Species Act, but the listing has not yet been given. The number of cutthroat trout is declining because its habitat has been destroyed by road building, timber harvesting, mining, and the construction of dams. Cutthroat trout have also bred with other species, resulting in fewer pure-bred cutthroats. The cutthroat trout is a favorite food for grizzly bears.

The cutthroat trout gets its name from the orange spot on its jaw which makes it look like it has been cut. The largest cutthroat on record was caught in 1955 and weighed 16 pounds.

STATE GRASS: BLUEBUNCH WHEATGRASS

Bluebunch wheatgrass became Montana's state grass in 1973. This grass grows throughout the state and provides excellent grazing for livestock.

STATE FOSSIL: DUCK-BILLED DINOSAUR

School children signed petitions and campaigned for Montana's newest state symbol, the duck-billed dinosaur. It became the official state fossil in 1985. Duck-billed dinosaurs lived 135 million years ago in what is now Montana. They had nests six feet in diameter

The duck-billed dinosaur was chosen as Montana's state fossil in order to draw attention to the state's important dinosaur discoveries.

with as many as twenty eggs. When newly hatched, the duck-billed dinosaur was less than fourteen inches long and weighed about one and a half pounds. Adults grew to more than 30 feet in length and weighed three tons.

STATE GEMS: SAPPHIRE AND AGATE

Montana **sapphire** and Montana agate became the state's official gemstones in 1969. Prospector Jake Hoover first found sapphires in Yogo Gulch in 1894. He gathered the blue pebbles and sent them in a cigar box to New York's Tiffany and Co. Tiffany's replied with a check for $3,750 and a letter describing the stones as "sapphires of unusual quality." Over the next 100 years, a string of short-lived mines produced nearly $25 million worth of sapphires. Agate, found in the eastern part of the state, is colorful. When polished, agate glistens with varying shades of brown, white, gray, and black.

Montana sapphire is found in every color of the rainbow. Montana agate is usually light yellow to almost clear in color.

Montana's History and People

Today, Montana's population reflects its Native American and European foundations. Historic and prehistoric sites help explain early Montana, the people who lived there, and the unique contributions they left.

EARLY PEOPLES

Artifacts show that some Native Americans, primarily the Kootenai, lived in the area now known as Montana more than 14,000 years ago. The majority of the area's Native Americans, though, arrived after 1700. Montana's plains were home to several Native American tribes, including the Arapaho, Assiniboine, Atsina, Blackfoot, Cheyenne, and Crow. The Bannack, Flathead, Kalispell, Kootenai, and Shoshone tribes lived in the mountains. Horses, introduced to Native Americans by Spaniards in the Southwest in the early 1600s, and guns, which came from white frontiersmen later in the century, played a major role in deciding which tribes would rule the Montana territory.

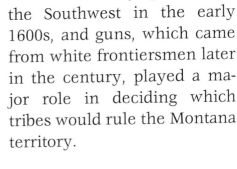

These are now seven Native American reservations in Montana. The first was established in 1851 for the Blackfoot.

EARLY EXPLORERS

There were no permanent European settlements in Montana until the 1800s. In 1803, the United States bought the Louisiana Territory from France for $15 million. The new territory included most of present-day Montana. President Thomas Jefferson decided he wanted to know more about this new territory. He asked his friend and former private secretary Meriwether Lewis to direct the exploration. Lewis asked his friend William Clark to help.

Lewis and Clark's group, called the Corps of Discovery, had about 33 members. Lewis and Clark met Sacajawea, a young Shoshone woman, when they were camped for the winter in what is now North Dakota. She acted as their interpreter. The Corps of Discovery traveled across Montana from April to September 1805. About 25 percent of the trail followed by the Corps of Discovery, almost 2,000 miles, is located in present-day Montana. Lewis and Clark were the first Europeans to see and write about many of the area's plants and animals.

The Fort Benton statue is Montana's official state memorial to Lewis, Clark, and Sacajawea.

After the Lewis and Clark expedition, many fur trappers and traders moved into the region. In 1847 the American Fur Company built Fort Benton as a trading post and military fort. It was located 40 miles northeast of present-day Great Falls, on the banks of the Missouri River. The town that formed around the fort, also known as Fort Benton, is Montana's oldest town.

THE MONTANA GOLD RUSH

In 1862 **prospectors** discovered gold in Grasshopper Creek, in southwest Montana. In 1863 and 1864 gold also was discovered at neighboring Bannack, Virginia City, Confederate Gulch, and Last Chance Gulch, which is now the city of Helena. The gold drew thousands of fortune seekers. Between 1880 and 1890, the population of Montana grew from about 39,000 to nearly 143,000.

In the 1870s, thousands of prospectors headed south from Helena to the area now known as Butte, where they discovered another valuable natural resource: copper. In the 1880s, Butte was the largest copper producer in the United States.

The railroad arrived in Montana in 1881. The railroad linked Montana with markets in the east and with the Pacific Ocean near Tacoma, Washington. The Northern Pacific Railroad made it possible to easily and quickly get mineral ore and other farming products to processing mills.

Marcus Daly and William A. Clark were the owners of the region's major mines. The two were friends when they first met but soon became rivals. When Clark bought the Butte newspaper and ordered his reporters to write nasty articles about Daly, Daly got revenge by starting his own newspaper.

More than 80,000 homesteaders moved into Montana between 1909 and the early 1920s.

OPENING THE WEST

The Free Homestead Act of 1862 gave 160 acres of land to anyone who promised to "prove up" the land. "Proving up" meant living on the land for five years. When the Free Homestead Act was passed, people rushed to stake their claims. In 1877 Congress passed the Desert Land Act. This act gave 640 acres, four times what the Free Homestead Act allowed, to anyone who irrigated the land within three years. In the first four years of this act, 370 desert farms were claimed in Montana Territory covering 122,000 acres.

Homesteaders often settled on land that belonged to Native American tribes. Native Americans depended heavily on the bison, using hides and hair to make shields, saddles, teepees, moccasins, pillows, and ropes. European settlers with fast horses and deadly guns found bison hunting to be a fun sport. The settlers and Native Americans often fought over the right to hunt bison. Two of the most famous Native American campaigns in U.S. history were fought in Montana Territory.

In 1876 two Native American chiefs, Sitting Bull and Crazy Horse, led a group of about 2,000 Sioux, Arapaho, and Northern Cheyenne warriors against Colonel George A. Custer's troops at the Battle of Little Bighorn. Custer had battled the tribes many times before, but this time his 260 troops were far outnumbered. Sioux lookouts saw Custer's men approaching their camp. Within just a few minutes the warriors defeated Custer's troops, killing all his soldiers. This was the biggest defeat of the U.S. Army by Native Americans, and it changed the way politicians and military leaders thought of them.

The last major battle in Montana began when the U.S. government tried to move the Nez Perce from their home in Oregon. Chief Joseph led the Nez Perce people through Montana, toward Canada. Nez Perce warriors and

The Sioux and Cheyenne took less than an hour to defeat Custer at Little Bighorn.

Chief Joseph made two trips to Washington, D.C., to plead directly to President Theodore Roosevelt for his people to return to their home.

U.S. soldiers fought for two days at Big Hole in southwestern Montana. Chief Joseph surrendered to Colonel Nelson Miles in October 1877 to save his people from further suffering. The leaders agreed the Nez Perce would be given blankets and other supplies they needed if they would move onto the Lapwai **Reservation.** The Nez Perce went to Indian Territory in Oklahoma while the government decided what to do with the tribe. Colonel Nelson argued that in the interest of future peace with the Native Americans, they should be treated with respect. He helped Chief Joseph move his followers onto the Lapwai and Colville reservations.

STATEHOOD

On May 26, 1864, President Abraham Lincoln signed an act making Montana a U.S. territory. It remained a territory for 25 years. Montanans longed for statehood, but to achieve it they needed to prepare a written constitution which Congress could approve. In 1889 Congress passed a law that made it possible for the people of North Dakota, South Dakota, Montana, and Washington to form constitutions and state governments and to be admitted into the Union on an equal basis with the original states. The citizens of Montana quickly adopted a constitution, and President Benjamin Harrison declared it the country's 41st state on November 8, 1889.

FAMOUS PEOPLE

Plenty Coups (1848–1932), Crow chief. Plenty Coups was the last and perhaps greatest chief of the Crow. His name, Chie Aleck-chea-ahoosh, when translated to English means "Many Achievements" or "Plenty Coups."

Gary Cooper (1901–1961), actor. Gary Cooper was born Frank James Cooper in Helena, Montana, on May 7, 1901. The actor made 92 films during his 35-year career. He won best-actor Oscars for *Sergeant York* and *High Noon*.

Norman MacLean (1902–1990), author. Norman Maclean was born in Iowa and his family moved to Missoula in 1909. Maclean earned his college degrees from Dartmouth and the University of Chicago, and he taught at both schools. While a teacher, Maclean wrote about nature, fishing, and other things that he had experienced while living in Montana. His best known books are *A River Runs Through It* and *Young Men and Fire*.

Mike Mansfield (1903–2001), politician. Mansfield was born in New York City. He went to live with relatives in Great Falls at age seven. At age fourteen, he lied about his age so he could enlist in the navy. He later served in the army and the marines. Mansfield eventually earned his high school diploma and college degrees. He was elected to the U.S. House of Representatives in 1942. He served five terms in the House and four terms in the U.S. Senate, becoming Senate Majority Leader in 1961. He is the longest-serving U.S. Senate Majority Leader in history.

Myrna Loy (1905–1993), actress. Myrna Williams Loy was born in Helena. She and her mother moved to California when her father died in 1917. Loy starred in silent films and talking movies. Her autobiography *Myrna Loy: Being and Becoming* was published in 1987.

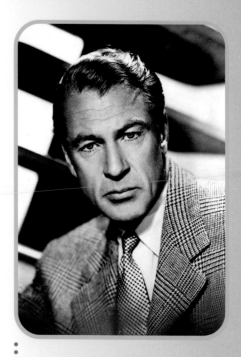

As a teenager, Gary Cooper walked in Yellowstone National Park as a tour guide.

Myrna Loy grew up on 5th Avenue in Helena, a few blocks from the Lewis and Clark County jail.

Evel Knievel's motorcycle is on display at the Museum of American History in Washington, D.C.

Dorothy Johnson (1905–1984), author. Dorothy M. Johnson was born in Iowa. Her widowed mother moved the family to Whitefish in 1913. In 1953, she began teaching journalism at the University of Montana. She is best known for her Western stories. Three of her books, *The Hanging Tree*, *Liberty Valance*, and *A Man Called Horse*, were made into movies.

Evel Knievel (1938–   ), daredevil motorcyclist. Evel Knievel was born in Butte. In 1965 he began his daredevil career with the Evel Knievel's Motorcycle Daredevils. On January 1, 1968, he jumped 151 feet across the fountains at Caesar's Palace in Las Vegas, but his landing was a disaster. His injuries put him in the hospital for 30 days. He later jumped across thirteen buses in London and the Snake River Canyon in the United States.

David Lynch (1946–   ), filmmaker. David Lynch was born in Missoula and spent his early years near Helena, where his father worked as a scientist for the Forest Service. He is perhaps best known for directing television's "Twin Peaks."

Dana Carvey (1955–   ), comedian. A Missoula native, Dana Carvey won the San Francisco Stand-Up Comedy Competition while in college. After graduation, he moved to Los Angeles to pursue his Emmy-winning comedy career. Carvey was a regular on "Saturday Night Live" for seven seasons beginning in 1986.

Pompey's Pillar

Along the entire Lewis and Clark trail, there is just one place where evidence of the explorers' presence still exists. That is Pompey's Pillar, a massive rock formation along the south bank of the Yellowstone River, about 30 miles east of Billings.

DISCOVERING AND PRESERVING THE PILLAR

Clark climbed the **butte,** looked out over the surrounding land, and carved his name and the date July 25, 1806, into the sandstone. He named the rock Pompey's Pillar for Sacajawea's son, Jean Baptiste Charbonneau, who was known as "Pomp."

Prospector James Stuart became the first person to see Clark's signature. James Stuart and his brother, Granville, made the territory's first gold strike in 1857 at Gold Creek. James Stuart saw the signature in 1863 when he led his gold prospecting party down the Yellowstone valley.

The Northern Pacific Railroad put an iron grate over the signature in 1882 to protect it from graffiti. In 1954 Don Foote, the pillar's last private owner, replaced the grate

Pompey's pillar stands 150 feet tall and is about 1,200 feet around at the base. Clark's name can still be seen carved into the rock.

with a brass and glass case that continues to protect the rock from weather and graffiti.

IMPORTANCE OF THE PILLAR

The pillar is important in Native American history as a landmark, lookout, and cultural site. It was used by the Sioux and Crow, who hunted buffalo on the Echata River. The Crow used the Pillar as a prayer site. The rock is decorated with Native American drawings. The Crow called the Pillar "The Place Where the Mountain Lion Lives" or "Mountain Lion's Lodge" because the north face of the Pillar is naturally shaped like the head of a lion.

Clark's signature is one of hundreds on the pillar. Some signatures date back to the 1870s, when the U.S. military passed through the area, and the 1880s, when the railroad was constructed.

VISITING THE PILLAR

In November 1991 the Foote family sold this natural historic landmark and the surrounding 473 acres to the Bureau of Land Management. Visitors can reach Clark's signature and an overlook on top of the pillar by climbing a wooden staircase. From the top of the butte you can see three mountain ranges: the Big Horns to the south, the Bull range to the northwest, and the Rocky Mountains to the west.

The Bureau of Land Management and Pompey's Pillar National Monument Association host Clark Day each July at the pillar.

The annual Clark Day celebration draws about 1,200 visitors and includes period costumes, a Crow **powwow,** *a buffalo burger cookout, and historic reenactments.*

Montana's State Government

Montana is governed by its constitution. A constitution is a plan of government. The state government is based in Helena and is modeled after the U.S. government. It has three branches: the legislative branch, the executive branch, and the judicial branch.

Executive Branch
Governor and Lt. Governor (four-year terms)
Carries out the laws of the state

Legislative Branch
House of Representatives 100 Representatives (2-year terms) / Senate 50 Senators (4-year terms)
Makes laws for the state

Judicial Branch
Supreme Court 7 Justices (8-year-terms)
District Courts 42 Judges (6-year terms)
Municipal Courts
Justice of the Peace Courts
Explains laws

Montana's capitol was dedicated in 1902.

LEGISLATIVE

Montana's legislature is made up of a Senate and House of Representatives. Each may propose a state law but both must pass it before it is sent to the governor for approval. The legislature may override a veto by the governor. The senate and house meet during odd-numbered years for up to 90 days.

The senate has 50 members who serve four-year terms. The House has 100 members who serve two-year terms. Legislators can serve up to eight years in any sixteen-year period. Each senator or representative serves a specific district, or area, of the state.

EXECUTIVE BRANCH

State government functioning is overseen by the executive branch. The head of this branch is the governor. He or she is elected by voters and serves a four-year term. Each governor may serve up to eight years during any sixteen-year period. The governor submits the state budget to the legislature and looks over **bills** proposed by the legislative branch. The governor can approve the bill and sign it into law, or **veto** it.

The governor also appoints members of boards and commissions who oversee the heads of state agencies and departments, such as the Board of Pardons and Paroles and the Board of Environmental Review.

Other officials also are part of the executive branch. The lieutenant governor fills in for the governor when necessary and takes on many special assignments such as traveling on trade missions. The secretary of state oversees elections, maintains a list of the state's registered voters, and tests voting machines. The attorney general is the state's chief law enforcement agent. The auditor works with government and citizens to make sure the state's money is properly spent. The superintendent of public instruction helps determine the state's educational policy. These officials are elected by voters and

Tribal Governments

Native American tribes have the right to develop their own form of government and establish their own laws. They are independent nations within a larger nation. The tribes can set up their own tribal police and court systems, regulate hunting, fishing, land use, and environmental pollution, and collect taxes. Tribal laws govern behavior of those living on or visiting a reservation.

There are seven federally recognized Native American nations in Montana. They are located on the Blackfoot Reservation, Crow Reservation, Flathead Reservation, Fort Belknap Reservation, Fort Peck Reservation, Northern Cheyenne Reservation, and Rocky Boy's Reservation. Some of these reservations are home to several tribes that work together to form a single nation. The state Office of Indian Affairs works with tribal leaders to make sure Native Americans understand the rights, privileges, and duties that go along with being citizens of Montana. However, members of these seven nations answer to the U.S. government, not the state.

Each tribal nation has its own tribal court system, much like the state of Montana's court system. On some reservations, judges are appointed. On others, they are elected. These courts rule on cases involving tribal members and those in which the crime took place on a reservation.

serve four-year terms. They may serve a maximum of eight years during each sixteen year period.

JUDICIAL BRANCH

The judicial branch interprets the laws. The state's judges settle legal disputes and, along with juries, determine the guilt or innocence of those accused of crimes.

Municipal courts and justice-of-the-peace courts handle local, less serious criminal cases such as shoplifting or speeding. Montana's 22 district courts serve as trial courts for all civil cases such as divorce or child custody. They also have more serious criminal cases, including armed robbery or car burglary. Each district has one to four judges, each elected to a six-year term.

In most states there is an intermediate, or **appellate** court, which reviews lower court rulings. Montana does not have an intermediate court. Lower court decisions are appealed directly to the Montana Supreme Court.

Justices of the Montana Supreme Court are asked to review more than 700 of the 30,000 cases filed each year at the District Court level. The court considers every case that is appealed to it. The cases often are reviewed by reading written briefs from the lower courts. The supreme court, which has a chief justice and six associate justices, hears oral arguments in about 40 cases per year.

Montana's Supreme Court justices for the 2003 court session from left to right: Patricia O'Brien Cottes, W. William Leaphart, James Regnier, Chief Justice Karla M. Gray, James Nelson, Jim Rice, and John Warner

Montana's Culture

Montana's heritage is closely tied to the state's farm-land, its mineral-rich mountains, and the many people who have called Montana home.

NATIVE AMERICAN POWWOWS

Montana's reservations are places where Native American culture can be experienced in sacred settings. Many tribes hold gatherings called **powwows** to celebrate tradition, friendship, and culture with singing, dancing, and socializing. At a powwow, guests enjoy Native American food and join tribal members in traditional dress for the Round Dance, a circle dance, where everyone holds hands. Black Elk, a member of the Oglala Sioux explained: "The power of the world always works in circles, and everything tries to be round. In the old days when we were a strong and happy people, all our power came to use from the sacred hoop of the nation, and so long as the hoop was unbroken, the people flourished." In this tradition, many aspects of a powwow have a circular theme.

The Crow Fair Powwow is the largest tribal celebration in the state, attracting about 45,000 participants each year. The fair in-

The six-day Crow Fair Powwow is held each August in Crow Agency by the Apsaalooke people of the Crow Reservation just south of Hardin.

cludes events such as Native American horse racing and rodeo, but the powwow draws visitors from around the world. It has been held for about 80 years. The daily parade procession is led by Native American war veterans and elders. Men wear traditional hip-high leggings, loin cloth, and moccasins. Women wear long deerskin dresses. Both men and women wear red face paint near their eyes, as protection from bad medicine and spirits.

Homesteaders

Homesteaders played an important role in settling Montana. Today, towns pay tribute to the homesteaders' hard work with annual celebrations. One of the most popular homesteading festivals is held each June in Scobey, in northeast Montana. Homesteaders flocked to Scobey in the early 1900s. Scobey's Pioneer Days and Antique Show features a family-oriented **vaudeville** show, traveling stage acts that were especially popular in the early 1900s. They often featured juggling, comedy routines, and animal acts. The three-day festival was started in 1967 and attracts about 2,000 visitors each year.

Running of the Sheep

Hundreds of sturdy Montana woolies charge down the main street of Reed Point, population 96, each Labor Day Weekend during the "Running of the Sheep." The event was inspired by 1989's Great Montana Centennial Cattle Drive, which celebrated Montana's statehood anniversary. But the sheep drive was more popular than the cattle drive, attracting about 12,000 people.

Montana's Food

You can find almost any type of food in Montana. Many of the most popular dishes, though, are those featuring ingredients from Montana, such as beef, lamb, catfish, wheat, and barley.

HUCKLEBERRIES

Plump, juicy, and bluish-black in color, huckleberries grow primarily in western Montana. Native Americans

Huckleberry Muffins

1 cup huckleberries

½ cup brown sugar

2 cups all-purpose flour

1 tablespoon baking powder

½ teaspoon salt

2 eggs

4 tablespoons margarine, melted

1 teaspoon vanilla

¼ cup milk

¼ cup corn syrup

Always have an adult help you when working with the oven!

Preheat oven to 450°F. Combine sugar and huckleberries. Stir in flour, baking powder and salt. In a separate bowl, beat together eggs, milk, vanilla, margarine, and syrup. Combine the two mixtures, using a fork to stir. Do not over mix. Fill well-greased muffin tins three quarters full. Bake for 20 to 25 minutes or until tops are golden.

33

used them for food, beverages, and dye. Grizzly bears like them too. The Native Americans used to watch where the bears browsed for berries, trusting the animals to show them the sweetest bushes. Twelve types of huckleberries grow in Montana and the surrounding states. Some produce bunches of berries, while others have single berries.

BEEF

Montana ranks sixth in the United States in beef production. Montanans are proud of their high-quality beef and enjoy preparing and eating it in a number of ways, from barbequing to roasting. Those who want to experience a truly unique Montana beef dish can attend a pitchfork fondue party. Cowboy chefs poke a big slab of steak on the end of a pitchfork and cook it in a huge kettle of hot oil. Pitchfork fondue is not something you will find in restaurants, but it is popular at festivals and at the state's many guest ranches.

Chuck wagons were used in the old west during long cattle drives. They provided food and comfort to cowboys who were often hundreds of miles from a town.

Chuck wagon-style cookouts also are favorites in Montana. Chuck wagons once accompanied ranchers on long cattle drives and served as kitchens and pantries on wheels. Traditional chuck wagon food includes ribs, burgers, beans, barbequed chicken, steaks, corn-on-the-cob, and home fries. A favorite chuck wagon dessert is apple slump. It is made by putting bread dough around the sides of an iron pot and filling the pot with apples and molasses, which is a thick, syrupy by-product of sugar refining. The slump is then cooked over an open fire.

Montana's Folklore and Legends

The word *folklore* describes the stories passed from **generation** to generation. Folklore explains how things came to be, how places or things got their names or why something is done a certain way. It also teaches a lesson.

THE FLATHEAD LAKE MONSTER

In 1889 western Montana's Flathead Lake was home to many passenger ships and steamers. Steamers or steam ships are large vessels powered by steam-driven propellers. One of these ships was the *U.S. Grant.* The ship's captain, James C. Kerr, saw a whale-like object in the water. Thinking of the safety of his ship and passengers, he watched the object closely. The captain quickly realized it was not another ship. Whatever it was, it was large, and clearly alive.

Flathead Lake is the largest fresh-water lake west of the Mississippi River. It is 28 miles long and up to 15 miles wide.

People still report seeing the creature today. In 1990, Montana's Fish, Wildlife and Parks Department began to keep track of the sightings. Locals and experts disagree over whether the Flathead Lake Monster is a serpent-like creature or a gigantic fish, but most agree that there really is something unusual out there in Flathead Lake.

Bitter Tears

Montana's state flower, Bitterroot, was an important food source for Montana Native Americans. Flathead Native Americans explain the name in the legend of an old woman crying bitter tears for her family, starving because buffalo were scarce and drought meant crops were difficult to grow. The Creator took pity on her and sent a spirit bird to tell her that a nourishing root would grow where each of her tears fell. As long as her people continued to respect and honor all of creation, the bird said, the root would come back each spring. And it does.

Montana's Sports Teams

Montana has no major professional teams, but athletics still are of great importance to Montanans. Montana has college sports teams and some minor league teams as well.

COLLEGE TEAMS

Missoula is home to the University of Montana Grizzlies. The university is part of the Big Sky Conference, a group of eight colleges that compete against each other in fifteen sports. The University of Montana has teams that compete in football, basketball, **cross country,** tennis, track and field, golf, soccer, and volleyball. The school's **mascot** is Monte the Grizzly, a motorcycle-riding, moonwalking bear. The University of Montana's football team has won two national championships in the NCAA I-AA Division, in 1995 and 2001.

Monte the Grizzly was named National Mascot of the Year in 2003. Monte is known for his dancing and back flips.

Montana State University (MSU) is located in Bozeman. Its athletic teams are known as the Bobcats, its mascot is Champ the Bobcat, and its school colors are gold and blue. MSU teams compete in football, basketball, volleyball, track and field,

Many Montana State University rodeo team members have gone on to find success on the professional rodeo circuit.

cross country, tennis, golf, and alpine and Nordic skiing. Men and women also compete in rodeo events including bareback bronco riding, calf roping, steer wrestling, and goat roping. MSU rodeo teams have won six men's national championships and one women's national championship.

North America's First Luge Run

The first luge run in North America was built at Lolo Hot Springs on western Montana's Lolo Pass in 1965. The 3,000-foot-long luge run is four-feet wide and was the site of the first American Luge Championships in February 1965.

Luge is a timed contest in which players travel feet-first on sleds down steep, curvy, ice-covered courses. A single luge sled weighs about 50 pounds (there are both single and double luge sleds). The slider steers with his or her legs and shoulders. Many luge competitors travel more than 65 miles an hour. Luge became an Olympic sport in 1964. At the time, the United States had no luge program, so the country sponsored a team of American soldiers who were stationed in Europe. Montana's luge run is still there, but it is now used for snowmobiling rather than luge competitions.

Montana's Businesses and Products

Natural resources are at the heart of Montana business. About 60 to 70 percent of Montana's economy is based on industries that rely on natural resources, mainly lumbering, farming, and mining.

AGRICULTURE

Montana agriculture generates more than $2 billion each year. The average Montana farm covers 2,714 acres. That's almost six-and-a-half times larger than the average-size U.S. farm. Montana ranks fourth among all states in both wheat and wool production. The state ranks sixth in sugar beets and eighth in production of both honey and alfalfa hay. There are 2.7 million cattle in Montana. The state has 432,000 sheep and lambs that annually produce about 4.1 million pounds of wool, or one-tenth of the country's total.

LUMBER AND WOOD PRODUCTS

Forests cover about one-fourth, or 22.4 million acres of Montana's land area. About 11,000 people work in Montana's forest-products industry.

More than three million acres of Montana's forests are reserved as national parks.

Sugar Beets

Montana ranks sixth in the nation in sugar beet production. Sugar beets are second only to sugarcane as a source of sugar. To get the sugar out of the beets, the beets are washed and cut into thin slices. The slices are put in hot water to draw out the sugar and form syrup. The syrup is then sent through a big, round filter to clean it. Finally it is dried to sugar, packaged and marketed.

Montana has two of the largest fifteen coal mines in the United States. Together they produce more than twenty million tons of coal a year.

MINING

Montana contains large deposits of two important fossil fuels, coal and petroleum. Mountain ranges in central, southern, and western Montana also contain large mineral deposits. Montana is the only U.S. producer of platinum and palladium, which is a metallic element used in the purification of hydrogen. The state is first in the production of talc, a whitish-gray mineral used to make powder, paint, and plastics. It is second in bentonite, a clay-like substance used to make cement and glue. It is fourth in lead and copper, and fifth in zinc and molybdenum, a gray metallic element used to make steel tougher.

TOURISM

Tourism and travel is Montana's largest and fastest-growing industry. About 9.5 million out-of-state travelers now visit the state each year. The state's top tourist attractions are Glacier National Park and Yellowstone National Park. Tourism adds more than $1.6 billion to the state's economy each year.

Attractions and Landmarks

When you say "Montana," people generally think about Yellowstone National Park and dude ranches. But there are many other things to do and see in Montana.

MUSEUMS

Charles M. Russell (1864–1926), one of the most famous artists to paint the West, spent much of his life in Montana. His work is shown at the Charles M. Russell Museum in Great Falls. In addition to more than 7,000 works of art, the museum has a hands-on gallery for children and collections of Native American artifacts.

The Museum of the Rockies in Bozeman features displays about **geology, paleontology,** and **archeology.** Geology is the study of the origin and structure of the earth. Paleontology is the study of fossils and ancient life forms. Archaeology is the science of recovering artifacts and learning from them.

In addition to Russell's work, the Charles M. Russell Museum features paintings by artists including O.C. Seltzer, E.I. Couse, and Henry Farny.

Places to see in Montana

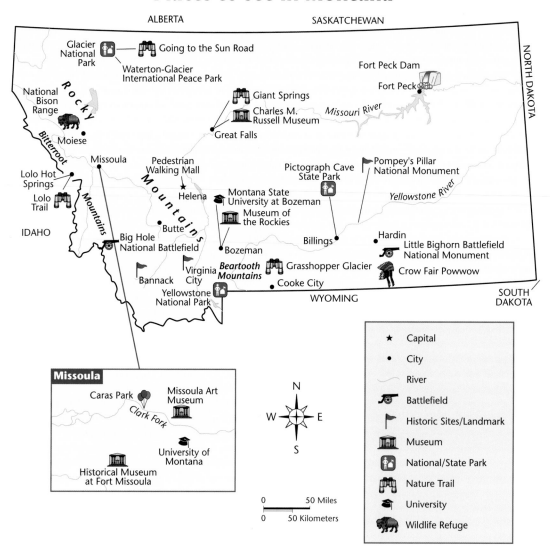

NATURE

Glacier National Park includes more than one million acres of forests, meadows, and lakes. The park has 700 miles of maintained trails that lead deep into one of the largest undamaged **ecosystems** in the lower United States. The park lies along Montana's northern border. In 1932 Glacier joined with Waterton Lakes National Park in Canada to form the Waterton-Glacier International Peace Park.

Grasshopper **Glacier** is located in the Beartooth Mountains near Cooke City. Grasshopper Glacier is 80 feet high, one mile long and a half-mile wide. It takes its name from the millions of now-extinct grasshoppers

An Engineering Feat: Building Going-to-the-Sun Road

Building Going-to-the-Sun Road was a huge challenge. Construction of the 52-mile road began in 1921. Workers relied on dirt trails to transport their supplies. They used horses and mules to pack their equipment. Two steam shovels, a gas shovel, drills, and explosives were used to build the road. The final part of the Going-to-the-Sun Road was completed in 1932 after eleven years of work.

The road is an outstanding example of "landscape engineering." It provides access to scenic areas without destroying the natural features. Going-to-the-Sun Road is the only road that crosses Glacier National Park. Travelers driving along the road enjoy views of scenic lakes, wildlife, and seasonal wildflowers.

that were trapped in its ice millions of years ago. The grasshopper mummies are still visible today.

Giant Springs is one of the largest freshwater springs in the world. The springs are located near Great Falls and were discovered by the Lewis and Clark Expedition in 1805. The spring produces about 338 million gallons of water each day. That's enough water to fill 1,336 Olympic size swimming pools!

HISTORIC ATTRACTIONS

Lolo Trail, also known as the Nez Perce Trail and the Lewis and Clark Trail, is an ancient Native American route across the Bitterroot Mountains. The Lewis and Clark expedition used the same trail when they traveled through Montana in 1805. In 1877, the Nez Perce used

During the late 1800s Virginia City was the most important city between Denver and San Francisco.

the trail to flee when the U.S. Army was trying to move them onto reservations.

Bannack is one of Montana's best preserved ghost towns. Gold was discovered in Grasshopper Creek in 1862. This set off a massive gold rush that increased tiny Bannack's population to more than 3,000 within one year. When the gold ran out, the town was abandoned.

Virginia City was founded in 1863 and quickly became home to thousands of fortune hunters during the 1880s and 1890s. The town was located in the midst of gold fields in southwest Montana. Virginia City became Montana's territorial capital in 1865. By the 1940s, it was almost a ghost town. History buffs Charlie and Sue Bovey visited Virginia City in the 1940s, and bought and fixed up the old buildings. Since then, Virginia City has become a major tourism destination.

Pictograph Cave State Park near Billings features paintings or **pictographs** that are more than 4,500 years old. Long before the arrival of the Crow or European settlers, ancient people used spears to hunt the woolly mammoth in Yellowstone Valley. The woolly mammoth was an Ice Age animal with long brown hair and curved ivory tusks that grew to the size of a present-day Asiatic elephant. These early hunters recorded their lives with paintings.

Pictograph Cave State Park has three main caves, Pictograph Cave, Middle Cave, and Ghost Cave, that were home to generations of prehistoric hunters.

Map of Montana

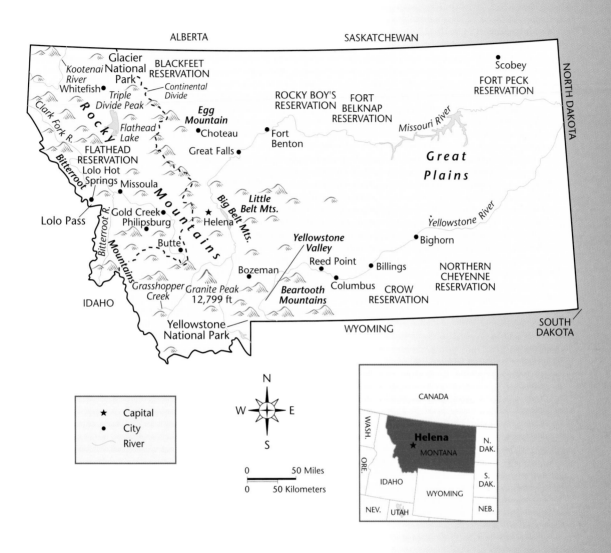

ALBERTA SASKATCHEWAN

Glacier
National
Park
Kootenai River
Whitefish
BLACKFEET RESERVATION
Continental Divide
Triple Divide Peak
Scobey
FORT PECK RESERVATION

NORTH DAKOTA

ROCKY BOY'S RESERVATION
FORT BELKNAP RESERVATION

Egg Mountain
Choteau
Fort Benton
Missouri River

Flathead Lake
Great Falls

Clark Fork R.

ROCKY

Great Plains

FLATHEAD RESERVATION
Lolo Hot Springs
Missoula

Bitterroot

Little Belt Mts.

Yellowstone River

Lolo Pass
Gold Creek
Philipsburg
Helena ★
Big Belt Mts.

Bighorn

Butte

Bitterroot R.
Mountains

Yellowstone Valley
Reed Point
Billings

NORTHERN CHEYENNE RESERVATION

Bozeman
Columbus
CROW RESERVATION

Mountains

Grasshopper Creek
Granite Peak 12,799 ft
Beartooth Mountains

IDAHO

Yellowstone National Park

SOUTH DAKOTA

WYOMING

★ Capital
• City
〜 River

N
W E
S

0   50 Miles
0   50 Kilometers

CANADA

WASH.
ORE.

Helena ★
MONTANA

N. DAK.

IDAHO

WYOMING

S. DAK.

NEV.   UTAH

NEB.

Glossary

appellate a court or judge that hears appeals and has the power to reverse lower court decisions

archaeology the scientific recovery and study of the remains of past human activities, such as burials, buildings, tools, and pottery

bills proposed laws

butte a steeply rising flat-topped hill

county seat a city or town that is the center of government in its county

cross country long-distance running events

ecosystems communities of plants, animals, and insects living within a particular environment

generation a group of people of the same basic age. Grandparents are one generation, your parents are the next generation, and you are the third generation

geology the science that studies the origin, history, and structure of the earth

geyser a hot spring that occasionally shoots water and steam into the air

glacier a large mass of ice slowly moving over a mountain or through a valley, formed over many years from packed snow in areas where snow falls faster than it melts

headwaters the waters from which rivers begin

homesteaders settlers who claimed land

mascot an athletic team's symbol or good luck charm

paleontology the scientific study of fossils and ancient forms of life

pictographs pictures representing words or ideas

powpow a meeting of Native Americans

prairie flat or rolling grassland

prospectors people who explore an area for a natural resource such as gold

reservation a piece of land set aside by the federal government for the use of Native Americans

sapphires any of several fairly pure forms of corundum, especially a blue form of the gem

territory a part of the United States not admitted as a state

threatened species a type of animal or plant that faces extinction

vaudeville stage entertainment offering a variety of short acts such as singing and dancing

veto right of the governor or president to reject a law passed by lawmakers

Victorian of, relating to, or belonging to the period of the reign of Queen Victoria from 1837 to 1901

World War I a war fought from 1914 to 1918, in which Great Britain, France, the United States, and their allies defeated Germany, Austria-Hungary, and their allies

World War II a war fought from 1939 to 1945, in which Great Britain, France, the Soviet Union, the United States, and their allies defeated Germany, Italy, and Japan

More Books to Read

Beaverhead, Pete and Woodcock, Clarence. *Mary Quequesah's Love Story: A Pend D'Oreille Indian Tale.* Helena: Montana Historical Society Press, 2001.

Kummer, Patricia K. *Montana: One Nation.* Minneapolis: Bridgestone Books, 1998.

Ladoux, Rita. *Montana.* Minneapolis, Minn.: Lerner Publishing Group, 2002.

Montana Historical Society. *Coyote Stories of the Montana Salish Indians.* Helena, Mont.: 1999.

Sateren, Shelley Swanson. *Montana Facts and Symbols.* Minnetonka, Minn.: Capstone Press, 2000.

Index

About the Author

Mary Boone lives in the Pacific Northwest and writes for publications such as *People, Teen People,* and *Seattle Homes and Lifestyles.* Missoula is her favorite city in Montana. She recommends everyone put Glacier National Park on their list of places to visit.